Grade 3

KUMON WRITING WORKBOOKS

Writing

W9-AYV-752

Table of Contents

KUMON

1 Trace the prefix. Then combine it with the word to create a new word.

5 points each

(1) _re_ + do = _redo_

(2) _un_ + tie = untie

(3) _sub_ + zero = subzero

(4) _mis_ + match = mismatch

(5) _pre_ + view = preview

(6) _dis_ + like = dislike

Don't forget!

A **prefix** is a group of letters, such as re-, un-, and sub-, that is added to the beginning of a word in order to form a new word.

For example: *preheat* means "to heat beforehand"

preview means "to view beforehand"

---

2 Complete each word with a prefix from the box.

5 points each

| sub | dis | mis | pre |

(1) mismatch

(2) subzero 0°C

(3) dislike

(4) preview

3 Make words with the puzzle pieces to match the pictures. You can use each piece more than once.

5 points each

re	un	load	wrap

(1) (unload)

(2) (reload)

(3) (unwrap)

(4) (rewrap)

4 Complete each sentence with a word from the brackets.

5 points each

(1) I must __untie__ my skates before I can take them off.

[untie / retie]

(2) She _____ basketball but likes soccer.

[dislikes / disinfects]

(3) We helped our mom _____ groceries from the car.

[unload / reload]

(4) Jeffrey made sure not to _____ any words in his essay.

[misbehave / misspell]

(5) We wore heavy coats to stay warm in the _____ temperatures.

[subgroup / subzero]

(6) Raymond has to _____ the oven before he puts in the pan.

[preheat / precook]

You're off to a great start!

2 Suffixes

Date   /   /

Name

Level ☆

Score   /100

1   Fill in each blank with the missing word.

5 points each

Word	+	Suffix	=	New Word
perfect	+	ly	=	perfectly
correct	+	ly	=	(1)
(2)	+	ly	=	loudly
quiet	+	ly	=	(3)
slow	+	ly	=	(4)
(5)	+	ly	=	swiftly

> **Don't forget!**
>
> A **suffix** is a letter or a group of letters added to the end of a word in order to form a new word.
> An **adverb** describes an action. Adverbs are usually formed by adding the -*ly* suffix to an adjective.
>   For example: She pets the kitten *gently*.

2   Complete the sentence pairs with an adjective and adverb from the box.

5 points each

> wild / wildly   cautious / cautiously   kind / kindly
>
> bright / brightly   anxious / anxiously

(1) The shopkeeper was _____.

He _____ let us try the ice-cream flavors.

(2) We were _____ on the steep steps.

We _____ held onto the rail.

(3) The horse was _____.

It _____ jumped and kicked.

(4) The car's lights are _____.

The lights _____ shine on the road.

(5) I was _____ about completing my test.

I _____ checked the time.

3 Answer each question with a phrase from the box.

| work busily | colors messily | builds skillfully |
| decorates carefully | steals greedily |

(1) What does the carpenter do?

The carpenter _____.

(2) What does the child do?

The child _____.

(3) What does the robber do?

The robber _____.

(4) What do the ants do?

The ants _____.

(5) What does the baker do?

The baker _____.

┌─ **Don't forget!** ─────────────────────────────────┐

If the word ends in a *y*, change the *y* to an *i* before adding the suffix *-ly*.
For example: *happy* becomes *happily*

└──┘

4 Change the word in the brackets to an adverb by adding the suffix *-ly*. Then complete each sentence with the adverb.

5 points each

(1) The art teacher _____ moved the wobbly sculpture.   [careful]

(2) The master violinist _____ played the song.   [skillful]

(3) His baby brother _____ played with finger paint.   [messy]

(4) The hungry dog _____ ate the food.   [greedy]

High five!

5

Suffixes

Level ☆

Score

/100

Date / /

Name

---

1 Trace the words to complete each sentence.

5 points each

(1) Look at all of the _colors_ in your dress. Your dress is _colorful_. Mine is _colorless_.

(2) The man held the antique with _care_. He was _careful_ because it was expensive. He was _careless_ with less valuable things.

(3) Some animals have _grace_. A giraffe is _graceful_. A hyena is _graceless_.

(4) The patient sent a card to _thank_ his doctor. This patient was _thankful_, but some patients are _thankless_.

> **Don't forget!**
>
> The suffix -*ful* means "full of."   For example: *fearful* means "full of fear"
> The suffix -*less* means "without."   For example: *fearless* means "without fear"

---

2 Complete each sentence with a word from the brackets.

5 points each

(1) The ballerina did _____ jumps.   [grace / graceful / graceless]

(2) The _____ firefighter saved the family.   [fear / fearful / fearless]

(3) Lei was _____ for her presents.   [thank / thankful / thankless]

(4) I held the newborn baby with _____.   [care / careful / careless]

3 Complete each sentence with a form of the word in the box. Add the suffixes *-er* or *-est* as needed.

6 points each

strong

(1) A donkey is ~~strong~~ .
A bear is ~~stronger~~ .
An elephant is the ~~strongest~~ .

young

(2) I am _____ .
My little brother is _____ than I.
Our baby sister is the _____ .

easy

(3) The hilly path is _____ to walk.
The flat path is _____ .
The downhill path is the _____ .

high

(4) The skateboarder jumps _____ .
The basketball player jumps _____ .
The skier jumps the _____ .

light

(5) Her suitcase is _____ .
His backpack is _____ .
Her purse is the _____ .

Don't forget!

The suffix *-er* means "more than." The suffix *-est* means "the most."

4 Complete each sentence with a word from the brackets.

6 points each

(1) We couldn't climb any _____ . We were at the _____ point.

[higher / highest]

(2) The cat was _____ but the kitten was _____ . [light / lighter]

(3) The test was _____ but was not the _____ . [easy / easiest]

(4) Ten _____ men competed. The _____ man won.

[strong / strongest]

(5) Diana is _____ than her sister.
Diana is the _____ in her family.

[younger / youngest]

You're getting better and better.

1 Trace the indefinite pronoun to complete each sentence.

5 points each

(1) Evan likes tennis and baseball.
He would like to play _either_ today.

(2) Even though she just ate an apple, she is still hungry.
She would like _another_ .

(3) I'm not sure if this book will be good.
Did _anyone_ read this book?

(4) Sonya is giving away her stickers.
Jeffrey would like _some_ .

(5) Art class was fun today. _Everyone_ painted sunflowers .

Don't forget!

An **indefinite pronoun** is a pronoun that refers to something that is not specific or exact.
For example: *all, anything, each, many,* and *nobody*

2 Write the indefinite pronoun in the space on the right.

5 points each

(1) Is anyone home?   (   )

(2) I biked with everyone to the pizza parlor.   (   )

(3) Oak Lane was straight, and Elm Drive was curvy.
Either would lead us home.   (   )

(4) He already had one sleeping bag, but he needed to
find another for his friend.   (   )

(5) Brian asked for more paper, and the teacher gave
him some.   (   )

3 Complete each answer with an indefinite pronoun from the box.

anyone	some	either	everyone	another

(1) "Did your cousin find the book she wanted?"

"No, but she found _____ that she likes."

(2) "Were your friends at the pool today?"

"No, _____ went to the movies because it rained."

(3) "Do you know any students in your new class?"

"I don't know _____."

(4) "Is there more lemonade?"

"Yes, there is _____ more."

(5) "Does Colleen like scary movies or funny movies?"

"She likes to watch _____."

4 Complete each sentence by replacing the bold words with an indefinite pronoun from the box.

either	everyone	another	some	anyone

(1) Today **Andrea, Michael, and April** hiked to the top of the mountain.

Today _____ hiked to the top of the mountain.

(2) I would like **one more pickle**, please.

I would like _____, please.

(3) Viviana took **a handful of beads** from the bowl.

Viviana took _____ from the bowl.

(4) The baby wanted **his bottle or his toy**.

The baby wanted _____.

(5) Did **you or Jamal** see which way the cat ran?

Did _____ see which way the cat ran?

Wow!

Punctuation
Speech

Level ☆

Score

/ 100

Date / /

Name

1 Trace the punctuation around the quotation in each sentence.

5 points each

(1) My best friend said __ __ I have so much fun when we're together __ __

(2) __ Good morning __ __ the principal said.

(3) __ Did you finish your homework ? __ our babysitter asked.

(4) __ Let's build an obstacle course __ __ Sean said.

(5) Grandpa asked __ __ How tall are you now ? __

Don't forget!

Quotation marks mark the beginning and end of a quotation. Pay attention to the location of the other punctuation, such as commas and periods, when using quotation marks.

For example: "I'm going to the zoo," said Denise.

---

2 Complete each sentence with punctuation.

5 points each

(1) Tommy said __ __ I would like to see the parade __ __

(2) The king asked __ __ Where is the queen __ __

(3) __ When are we leaving __ __ she asked.

(4) __ He lost his parents in the crowd __ __ the police officer said.

(5) __ I need a new tire for my bike __ __ Tyrone said.

3 Rewrite each sentence as direct speech.

5 points each

(1) Jonah said that he will miss practice.

Jonah said, "I will miss practice."

(2) The announcer said that there are only five tickets.

_____

(3) Leslie asked who is the new principal.

_____

(4) Pete said that these are his pet hamsters.

_____

4 Rewrite each sentence with punctuation and capitalization.

6 points each

(1) may I buy some tulips the man asked

"May I buy some tulips?" the man asked.

(2) rachel told me i sold muffins at the bake sale

_____

(3) mr. nielsen said the picnic starts at eleven o'clock

_____

(4) karen asked the coach can we practice slap shots

_____

(5) the club meets here she said

_____

I'm impressed!

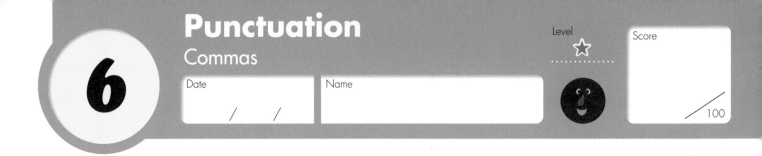

Punctuation
Commas

Level

Score
/ 100

Date   /   /

Name

1 Insert commas to separate the items in each series.

5 points each

(1) The musician could play guitar, piano, and bass.

(2) Colleen likes to read novels   short stories   and news articles.

(3) My favorite foods are watermelon   corn   and ice cream.

(4) My dad packed his suit   tie   shoes   and laptop for his business trip.

(5) Humans   mice   dolphins   and chimpanzees are all mammals.

Don't forget!

Commas separate items in a series. When a conjunction, such as *and* or *or*, joins the last two items in a series, a comma is used.

For example: I like to run, swim, and bike.

---

2 Combine the sentences with commas and the conjunction in the brackets.

5 points each

(1) She is not short. She is not strong. She is not fast.   [or]

She is not short, strong, or fast.

(2) Rita bought bread. Rita bought cheese. Rita bought tomatoes.   [and]

_____

(3) I visited Santa Fe. I visited Madison. I visited Little Rock.   [and]

_____

(4) Geckos are reptiles. Snakes are reptiles. Sea turtles are reptiles.   [and]

_____

(5) Daniel doesn't eat chips. He doesn't eat soda. He doesn't eat chocolate.   [or]

_____

3 Combine the sentences with a comma and a conjunction from the brackets.

5 points each

(1) Justin earned $115 this summer. He bought a scooter. [and / but]

Justin earned $115 this summer, and he bought a scooter.

(2) We closed the window. The flies were already inside. [so / but]

We closed the window _____.

(3) She liked playing soccer. She joined a team. [so / yet]

She liked playing soccer _____.

(4) The sculpture was done. The clay was not dry. [but / and]

The sculpture was done _____.

(5) The bus stopped. The man didn't get on it. [and / yet]

The bus stopped _____.

Don't forget!

A **simple sentence** has a noun, verb, and object. A comma and a conjunction can join two simple sentences.

For example: Mary played the guitar, but Ezra didn't sing.

---

4 Combine the sentences with a comma and a conjunction from the box.

5 points each

| and | or | so | yet | but |

(1) I will win. It will be a tie.

_____

(2) Birds must protect their chicks. They stay near their nests.

_____

(3) The man walked the dog. The woman trained it.

_____

(4) The store had books to sell. There were no customers.

_____

(5) He told me to wait. I left anyway.

_____

Good going.

7

Level ☆

Score
/100

Date   /   /

Name

1 Trace the apostrophe and *s* to complete each sentence. Then read each sentence aloud.

5 points each

(1) Robin __'s__ lasagna recipe is wonderful.

(2) We looked at the artist __'s__ canvas as he painted.

(3) That is Raymond __'s__ backpack.

(4) The Olympic Games are the world __'s__ biggest sporting event.

(5) It was raining, so Jamie __'s__ practice was canceled.

Don't forget!

An **apostrophe** and *s* (*'s*) at the end of a word shows ownership.

For example: Harold's crayon is purple.

(The crayon belongs to Harold.)

---

2 Write an apostrophe and *s* at the end of each word to show ownership. Then read each sentence aloud.

5 points each

(1) My mom ____ car is old, but it runs well.

(2) Gabriela ____ knee pads were dirty.

(3) The old woman ____ cane was made of wood.

(4) My uncle ____ wedding ring is gold.

(5) The doctor ____ thermometer was in his hand.

3 Rewrite each sentence with the subject in possessive form.

5 points each

(1) The mailman has thick glasses.

The mailman's glasses are thick.

(2) The tourist has comfortable sneakers.

_____

(3) The captain has a blue ferry.

_____

(4) Allan has a birdhouse outside.

_____

(5) Ellen has a job at a camp.

_____

4 Answer the question according to the picture. Write each sentence with the subject in the possessive form.

5 points each

(1) Whose lunch bag is that?

That is Prateek's lunch bag.

(2) Whose books are those?

_____

(3) Whose volleyball is that?

_____

(4) Whose backpack is that?

_____

(5) Whose rain boots are those?

_____

Prateek	Raymond
Ellen	Megan
Ryan	Louis

Good for you.

Review
Punctuation

8

Level ☆

Score

Date   /   /

Name

/100

1 Rewrite each sentence as direct speech with punctuation and capitalization.

5 points each

(1) georgia said I like your comic

_____

(2) my teacher said please be on time

_____

(3) will you call the king the queen asked

_____

(4) a hurricane is on the way the news anchor reported

_____

(5) grandma asked did you like this book

_____

2 Combine the sentences with a comma and a conjunction from the brackets.

5 points each

(1) We will eat leftovers. Dad will order pizza.   [yet / or]
We will eat leftovers _____.

(2) I practiced my speech many times. I was still nervous.   [yet / so]
I practiced my speech many times _____.

(3) The dog likes to play with his ball. He is tired now.   [but / or]
The dog likes to play with his ball _____.

(4) School is starting soon. We will need supplies.   [so / but]
School is starting soon _____.

(5) Anita carried the bags inside. Micah unpacked them.   [and / or]
Anita carried the bags inside _____.

3 Rewrite each sentence with the subject in possessive form.

6 points each

(1) The janitor has a wet mop.

The janitor's mop is wet.

(2) The figure skater has a beautiful costume.

_____

(3) My cousin has a red rosebush.

_____

(4) Amy has a large apron.

_____

(5) The basketball player has an important game.

_____

4 Rewrite each sentence with capitalization and punctuation.

5 points each

(1) the farmer sold berries and his son sold lemons

_____

(2) did you hear the news karen asked

_____

(3) a ballerinas pointe shoes help her stand on her toes

_____

(4) the science clubs projects are on display the principal said

_____

Fantastic!

9

Subject / Predicate
Review

Level ☆

Date / /

Name

Score /100

1 Complete each sentence with a subject and predicate from the boxes.

6 points each

Subjects

A bandit	Jess and Ed
The birds	
Ms. Alvarez	My brother

Predicates

baked ten cookies　　stole the horse

taught me fractions

escape from the cage　　tossed a ball

(1) __The birds__ __escape from the cage__ .

(2) _____ _____ .

(3) _____ _____ .

(4) _____ _____ .

(5) _____ _____ .

2 Rewrite each sentence using the adjective in the brackets to describe the subject.

5 points each

(1) The gardener lifted the branches. [powerful]

__The powerful gardener lifted the branches.__

(2) The scientist showed his invention. [clever]

_____

(3) Alice's kite is tangled in the tree. [colorful]

_____

(4) The alarm hurts my ears. [blaring]

_____

3 Write the subject of each sentence in the space below.

5 points each

(1) The trick-or-treaters put on their costumes.

_____

(2) My pink gloves are dirty.

_____

(3) A graceful giraffe ran across the plains.

_____

(4) The jubilant team cheered when their teammate hit a home run.

_____

(5) Our cautious bus driver watched the road carefully.

_____

4 Write the predicate of each sentence in the space below.

5 points each

(1) Elijah passed me the vegetables.

_____

(2) The elderly woman shopped at the market.

_____

(3) The butler lit a candle and led the guests.

_____

(4) The cows wandered on the hill.

_____

(5) A plastic bag littered the beach.

_____

You did great!

Subject / Predicate
Review

10

Level

Score

/100

Date   /   /

Name

1 Complete the predicate of each sentence with an adverb from the brackets.

5 points each

(1) The wizard laughed _____ about his evil plan.   [gleefully / correctly]

(2) He laid the clothes _____ to dry.   [nowhere / everywhere]

(3) Juliette _____ finished the race.   [easily / before]

(4) We stood _____ from the fire.   [close / far]

(5) I will celebrate my birthday _____.   [today / during]

2 Write the predicate of each sentence in the space below.

5 points each

(1) I went to the bathroom to carefully wash my hands.

went to the bathroom to carefully

wash my hands

(2) The golfer briskly walked to his golf ball.

_____

(3) My mom kindheartedly made me soup when I was sick.

_____

_____

(4) Joni nervously walked to the piano to perform at the recital.

_____

_____

(5) The librarian silently put the books on the shelf.

_____

3 Complete each sentence with a predicate from the box. 6 points each

| rapidly ran after the elephant knew every answer on the science test |
| accidentally spilled his drink |
| stayed up late to watch the stars is turning nine years old soon |

(1) The lion _____ .

(2) I _____ .

(3) Rose _____ .

(4) My brother _____ .

(5) We _____ .

4 Circle the subject. Then write the predicate in the space below. 5 points each

(1) (An adventurous fish) swam through the ocean.

_____

(2) The bland potatoes stuck to the top of his mouth.

_____

(3) Jed energetically ran to catch the ice-cream truck.

_____

(4) The eager dog impatiently waited for some scraps.

_____

Bravo!

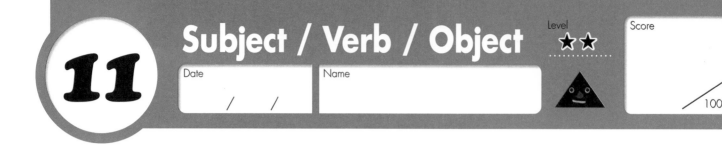

11 Subject / Verb / Object

Level ★★

Date / /

Name

Score /100

1 Circle the subject, underline the verb, and then write the remaining words in the space provided.

5 points each

(1) (Stacey) plays the accordion.   the accordion

(2) The worker constructs a home.   _____

(3) My mom made a pie.   _____

(4) We watch the acrobats.   _____

(5) The bear caught a fish.   _____

Don't forget!

The **object** is the thing or person on which the subject acts. To find the object, ask who or what the subject acts upon.

For example: Tamra   rode   the express train.
subject   verb   object

What did Tamra ride? The express train.

---

2 Write the subject, verb, and object of each sentence in the chart.

5 points each

Subject	Verb	Object

(1) The ball shattered the window.

(2) I ignored the bully.

(3) Matt trained his dog.

(4) The president wrote a letter.

3 Write a sentence with the words in the brackets. Begin each sentence with a capital letter.

5 points each

(1) [borrowed / a pencil / the teacher]

The teacher _____ borrowed _____ a pencil _____.
subject   verb   object

(2) [ride / the carousel / we]

_____ _____ _____.
subject   verb   object

(3) [the curb / the car / hit]

_____ _____ _____.
subject   verb   object

(4) [my doctor / my wound / treated]

_____ _____ _____.
subject   verb   object

(5) [seashells / collected / the friends]

_____ _____ _____.
subject   verb   object

4 Complete the answer to each question.

6 points each

(1) What is Kate carrying?

Kate _____ is carrying _____ an umbrella _____.
subject   verb   object

(2) What is the man riding?

_____ is riding _____.
subject   verb   object

(3) What is Min writing?

Min _____ an invitation.
subject   verb   object

(4) What is the girl wearing?

_____ is wearing _____.
subject   verb   object

(5) What are the boys trading?

_____ _____ _____.
subject   verb   object

Nice baseball card!

Incredible!

1 Write the subject, verb, and object of each sentence.

6 points each

(1) Doug and the coach brought the bats.

<u>Doug and the coach</u>   <u>brought</u>   <u>the bats</u>
subject   verb   object

(2) The tall woman rode a motorcycle.

_____   _____   _____
subject   verb   object

(3) The famous athlete fractured her arm.

_____   _____   _____
subject   verb   object

(4) Her husband cooked her dinner.

_____   _____   _____
subject   verb   object

(5) Marie and her friend moved the wardrobe.

_____   _____   _____
subject   verb   object

2 Write the object of each sentence.

6 points each

(1) A park ranger protects the forest.   <u>the forest</u>

(2) Max picked the carrots.   _____

(3) The tourist held a camera.   _____

(4) My uncle barbecued the eggplant.   _____

(5) The nurse signed the paper.   _____

3 Write the subject or object of each sentence as indicated. 5 points each

(1) Sophie and her mom wear sunblock and hats.

_____sunblock and hats_____
object

(2) The enormous octopus attacks its prey.

_____
subject

(3) The shaggy camel carried a woman and two bags.

_____
object

(4) Carrie and Ryan purchased elegant stationery.

_____
subject

4 Complete each answer with an object from the box. 5 points each

a hose	tomatoes	her lunch	a clue

(1) What did Tammy cut yesterday?

Tammy _cut_ _tomatoes_ yesterday.
subject   verb   object

(2) What did the firefighter carry?

_____ _____ _____.
subject   verb   object

(3) What did Ava take to school?

_____ _____ _____ to school.
subject   verb   object

(4) What did the detective find?

_____ _____ _____.
subject   verb   object

Remarkable work.

Subject and Verb Agreement

Level ★★

1 Complete each sentence with a verb from the brackets.

5 points each

(1) Stephanie and Kristen _____ the flute.   [practice / practices]

(2) The magician _____ a rabbit from his hat.   [pull / pulls]

(3) All the teachers, except for Mr. Becker, _____ in the meeting.   [are / is]

(4) Giant pandas _____ twelve hours a day eating.   [spend / spends]

(5) The puck, with a coupon, _____ ten dollars.   [cost / costs]

> **Don't forget!**
>
> If the subject is singular, the verb must be singular. If the subject is plural, the verb must be plural.

2 Complete each sentence with a subject from the brackets.

5 points each

(1) In the movie, an _____ lands on earth.

[alien / aliens]

(2) The _____ rehearses today.

[actor / actors]

(3) The _____ run with the riders on their backs.

[horse / horses]

(4) Each _____ has a unique pattern and color.

[feather / feathers]

3 Complete each sentence with a verb from the brackets. 5 points each

(1) I _____ a third grader. They _____ second graders.

    [am / are / is]   [am / are / is]

(2) They _____ on a class trip, but he _____ home sick.

     [am / are / is]   [am / are / is]

(3) She _____ playing the piano while we _____ singing along.

     [am / are / is]   [am / are / is]

(4) _____ you crying because it _____ a sad play?

    [am / are / is]   [am / are / is]

4 Complete each sentence with a verb from the brackets. 5 points each

(1) Both Hernando and Caitlin _____ the car.

                          [wash / washes]

(2) A plane and a car _____ gas to fuel their engines.

                          [use / uses]

(3) The delivery person _____ a package.

                          [drop / drops]

(4) Either the author or the illustrator _____ the book.

                          [sign / signs]

(5) The stream and the pond _____ sometimes.

                          [overflow / overflows]

(6) The children _____ ninjas when they put on costumes.

                          [become / becomes]

(7) _____ Mexican or Italian your favorite cuisine?   [is / are]

You are a star!

14 Subject and Verb Agreement

Level ★★

Date / /

Name

Score /100

1 Trace the subject. Then read each sentence aloud.

15 points for completion

Singular subjects

Each person runs.

Everyone runs.

Somebody runs.

No one runs.

Anybody runs.

Plural subjects

Both people run.

Several people run.

Few people run.

Many people run.

2 Complete each sentence with a verb from the brackets.

5 points each

(1) Both David and Jimmy _____ karate.   [know / knows]

(2) Each apple _____ if it is not eaten.   [rot / rots]

(3) Somebody _____ the building before it is built.   [sketch / sketches]

(4) Many cheerleaders _____ in competitions.   [perform / performs]

(5) Does anybody _____ to visit the beach with me?   [want / wants]

(6) Several windmills _____ damaged during the storm.   [was / were]

(7) Everyone _____ that the food is burning!   [realize / realizes]

(8) Few people _____ in the Olympics.   [compete / competes]

3 Complete each sentence with a verb from the brackets.

(1) Many customers _____ waiting for the store to open.

[are / is]

(2) Few people _____ able to make extraordinary discoveries.

[are / is]

(3) Somebody _____ performing on the balance beam.

[are / is]

(4) Everyone _____ going fishing on Saturday morning.

[are / is]

(5) Several merchants _____ selling T-shirts at the concert.

[are / is]

(6) No one _____ daydreaming during Mr. Thomas's class.

[are / is]

(7) Each math question _____ challenging.

[are / is]

(8) An enormous elephant _____ bathing in the river.

[are / is]

(9) Anybody _____ free to try out for the school musical.

[are / is]

You are the best!

Verbs
Past Tense

1 Complete each sentence with the past tense of the verb in the brackets.

5 points each

(1) Yesterday the magician _____ his magic trick.

[show]

(2) The boy _____ in his friend's ear.

[whisper]

(3) Jennifer carefully _____ the gift for her grandmother.

[wrap]

(4) My sister _____ a patch onto her jeans.

[sew]

(5) Our family _____ from drinking soda to drinking water.

[switch]

2 Complete each sentence with a verb from the brackets.

5 points each

(1) Earlier today, the clerk _____ the customer's change.

[count / counts / counted]

(2) We used our passports when we _____ last summer.

[travel / travels / traveled]

(3) The band _____ its concert last night by taking a bow.

[end / ends / ended]

(4) The bird _____ over the water and dove in when it saw a fish.

[hover / hovers / hovered]

(5) At our last summer party, fireflies _____ in the front yard at dusk.

[glow / glows / glowed]

3 Complete the chart. 10 points for completion

Present	Past
wipe / wipes	wiped
tickle / tickles	_____
_____ / shaves	shaved
measure / measures	_____
compete / competes	_____

4 Complete each sentence with the present or past tense of the verb. 8 points each

(1) [wipe]

    a) Yesterday, the man ___wiped___ the counter with soap and water.

    b) Don't ___wipe___ your hands on your pants.

(2) [shave]

    a) Yesterday, my cousin _____ his face for the first time.

    b) The pastry chef _____ off pieces of chocolate for the cake.

(3) [tickle]

    a) My dad _____ me, and I laughed.

    b) The baby's aunt _____ her feet every time they are together.

(4) [measure]

    a) When the nurse _____ me last year, I was four feet tall.

    b) Can you _____ the flour for the recipe?

(5) [compete]

    a) As a child, he _____ in many track meets.

    b) The math team _____ each year and wins.

You made it!

Irregular Verbs
Past Tense

16

Level ★★

Score /100

Date / /

Name

1 Complete each sentence with the past tense of the verb in the brackets.

5 points each

(1) I __multiplied__ the numbers for my assignment.

[multiply]

(2) Yuri's baby sister _____ all night long.

[cry]

(3) The pilot _____ his luggage for his trip.

[carry]

(4) Yesterday, my mom _____ the living room.

[tidy]

(5) We formed a group and _____ for the science test.

[study]

2 Complete each sentence with a verb from the brackets.

5 points each

(1) Last night, a delivery person _____ pizza to the house.

[carry / carried]

(2) If you _____ fourteen by two, you will get the answer.

[multiply / multiplied]

(3) Don't _____. It will be all right.

[cry / cried]

(4) Last week, our class _____ how plants use sunlight for food.

[study / studied]

(5) "Please _____ your room," my mother requested.

[tidy / tidied]

3 Complete the chart.

10 points for completion

Present	Past
sweep / sweeps	swept
sleep / sleeps	slept
meet / meets	met
feel / feels	felt
creep / creeps	crept

4 Complete each sentence with the present or past tense of the verb.

8 points each

(1) [meet]

   a) The couple _met_ when they walked their dogs in the park.

   b) Come _meet_ our new neighbors.

(2) [sleep]

   a) When Latanya was a baby, she _____ in a crib.

   b) Bears _____ throughout winter.

(3) [feel]

   a) She remembered that the doctor _____ for any broken bones.

   b) I _____ tired if I don't get to bed on time.

(4) [sweep]

   a) Yesterday, the doorman _____ the walkway.

   b) Workers always _____ the road after a ticker tape parade.

(5) [creep]

   a) Earlier, the kids _____ up to the classroom window and peeked in.

   b) Please don't _____ around and scare me!

You're sharp!

Irregular Verbs
Past Tense

17

Level ★★

Score

Date   /   /

Name

/100

1 Complete each sentence with the past tense of the verb in the brackets.

5 points each

(1) Yesterday, the dog ___dug___ a hole and hid his bone.

[dig]

(2) The ice-skater _____ around gracefully.

[spin]

(3) The golfer _____ his club and hit the ball into the hole.

[swing]

(4) She _____ her favorite stickers all over her notebook.

[stick]

(5) My father _____ the family portrait above our fireplace.

[hang]

2 Complete each sentence with a verb from the brackets.

5 points each

(1) Please don't _____ your gum under the desk.

[stick / stuck]

(2) If we _____ down far enough, we will hit the buried treasure.

[dig / dug]

(3) Earlier, the principal _____ the banner to welcome the parents.

[hangs / hung]

(4) The gate _____ open during last night's storm.

[swing / swung]

(5) Look at him _____ the basketball on his finger.

[spin / spun]

3 Complete the chart.

10 points for completion

Present	Past
hurt / hurts	hurt
put / puts	put
spread / spreads	_____
cost / costs	_____
burst / bursts	_____

4 Complete each sentence with the present or past tense of the verb.

8 points each

(1) [spread]

   a) This morning, my sister _____ jam on her toast.

   b) The boys _____ the map out on the table to see the route.

(2) [cost]

   a) The shirt _____ too much money, so we returned it.

   b) How much does the toy _____?

(3) [put]

   a) Last night, my mother _____ beans into the slow cooker.

   b) The trained dogs _____ their toys down and sit still.

(4) [hurt]

   a) Last summer, my cousin _____ his leg while waterskiing.

   b) Don't _____ yourself while playing football.

(5) [burst]

   a) When her ice-cream cone fell, the child _____ into tears.

   b) Water balloons _____ if we throw them.

You got it!

Irregular Verbs
Past Tense

18

Level ★★

Score

Date / /

Name

/100

1 Complete each sentence with the past tense of the verb in the brackets.

5 points each

(1) She _____ writing in her workbook, but now she is finished.

[is]

(2) The binoculars _____ in the drawer, but now they are on the desk.

[are]

(3) I _____ dressed as a wizard, but now I am in my regular clothes.

[am]

(4) They _____ training exercises, so now they stretch.

[do]

(5) We _____ an old car that broke down, so now we have a new one.

[have]

2 Complete each sentence with a verb from the brackets.

5 points each

(1) The spacecraft _____ exploring outer space until last fall.

[is / am / was]

(2) We _____ busy today because the school play is tomorrow.

[is / are / was]

(3) While the boat floated nearby, the scuba divers _____ in the water.

[is / are / were]

(4) Last night, the comedian _____ a funny impression of the president.

[do / did]

(5) John _____ a viola lesson in the music room soon.

[have / has / had]

3 Complete the chart.

Present	Past
am	_____
is	_____
do	_____
has / have	_____
are	_____

4 Complete each sentence with the present or past tense of the verb in the brackets.

8 points each

(1) [have]

    a) Tommy ___had___ ten gumballs, but then he ate two.

    b) The three opera singers ___have___ a concert now.

(2) [is]

    a) A butterfly _____ flying nearby earlier.

    b) The teacher _____ writing our homework on the board now.

(3) [are]

    a) The passengers _____ seasick before the waters became calm.

    b) The teammates _____ running the relay race now.

(4) [do]

    a) The ladies _____ their hair for the ball last night.

    b) Please _____ your chores before you go outside to play.

(5) [am]

    a) I _____ in the spelling bee last year.

    b) I _____ in the third grade now.

Take a bow!

Date   /   /

Name

1 Complete each sentence with words from the box.

5 points each

are watching	are riding	is sleeping	am licking

(1) Ginny _____ in her room.

(2) I _____ my lollipop.

(3) We _____ in our little green wagon.

(4) They _____ a movie.

Don't forget!

Verbs in the **present progressive tense** describe actions that are happening now. To write in the present progressive tense, use the present tense of the helping verb *to be* and the present participle, or *-ing* form, of the main verb.

For example: She ⓘⓢ walking up the hill.

singular present   present participle of *walk*
form of *to be*

---

2 Complete each sentence with the present participle of the verb in the brackets.

5 points each

(1) The children are __going__ to school.   [go]

(2) I am _____ my favorite book.   [read]

(3) Athena is _____ a vegetable garden.   [plant]

(4) The puppies are _____ in the backyard.   [play]

3 Complete each sentence with words from the brackets.

6 points each

（1） Maggie _____ a book.   [are reading / is reading]

（2） We _____ home right now.   [are going / is going]

（3） I _____ to you.   [is talking / am talking]

（4） Brody _____ a song.   [is singing / are singing]

（5） They _____ letters to each other.   [is writing / are writing]

4 Complete each sentence with a phrase from the box.

6 points each

are riding our bicycles home   are having a barbecue
am redoing my messy homework
is checking our book reports   is running a marathon

（1） The teacher _____.

（2） My friends and I _____.

（3） I _____.

（4） The neighbors _____.

（5） She _____.

You are doing great!

Verbs
Present Progressive

Level ⭐⭐

Score

/100

Date　/　/

Name

1 Complete each sentence with a helping verb and the present participle of the verb in the brackets.

5 points each

(1) I __am walking__ in the park. [walk]

(2) Lila __is_____ on her computer. [work]

(3) They __are_____ for the home team. [cheer]

(4) My baby sister __is_____ loudly. [cry]

2 Rewrite each sentence in the negative present progressive form.

10 points each

(1) I am singing with the choir tonight. [not]

I am not singing with the choir tonight.

(2) Annika is playing in the championship. [not]

_____

(3) They are sitting in the theater. [not]

_____

(4) The baker is baking cupcakes. [not]

_____

3 Write a question based on each answer. 4 points each

(1) ___Are___ you _____ to me?

I am listening to you.

(2) _____ you _____ carefully?

I am working carefully.

(3) _____ he _____ nicely to you?

He is speaking nicely to me.

(4) _____ I _____ this work correctly?

You are doing this work correctly.

4 Complete each sentence with a helping verb from the box. You can use each helping verb more than once. 4 points each

are	am	is

(1) _____ Max and Emma hiking today?

(2) It _____ snowing harder this morning.

(3) You _____ not going to have more homework.

(4) _____ I going with you to the store?

(5) Anders _____ going to the beach tomorrow.

(6) I _____ reading my younger sister a story.

Neat work!

Verbs
Future Tense

21

Level ★★

Score

Date / /

Name

/100

1 Trace the helping verb and main verb to complete each sentence.

5 points each

(1) I __will send__ an e-mail to my teacher later.

(2) Mom __will think__ our artwork is wonderful when we finish it.

(3) The workers __will lay__ the foundation once the cement is mixed.

(4) You __will work__ harder on your next assignment to get a better grade.

Don't forget!

Verbs in the **future tense** describe an event that has not happened yet. To write in the future tense, use the helping verb *will* in front of the main verb.

For example: Jenee (will) [write] a story about butterflies.

helping verb　　main verb
---

2 Trace the helping verb. Then complete each sentence with a verb from the box.

6 points each

arrive	practice	bake	drive	build

　　　　　　　　　　helping verb　　　main verb

(1) Sami __will__ __practice__ his multiplication tables tonight.

(2) You __will__ _____ a dollhouse tomorrow.

(3) The announcer __will__ _____ at the stadium early.

(4) They __will__ _____ on the highway.

(5) Mom and I __will__ _____ chocolate cookies later.

3 Complete each answer with the verb in the future tense.

5 points each

(1) Will you play checkers with me?

Yes, I _____ checkers with you.

(2) Will Aunt Ana eat dinner with us?

No, Aunt Ana _____ not _____ dinner with us.

(3) Will they sing songs at the celebration?

Yes, they _____ songs at the celebration.

(4) Will Malik take his bicycle to school?

No, Malik _____ not _____ his bicycle to school.

4 Rewrite each sentence in the future tense.

6 points each

(1) Raj goes to the bus stop.

Raj will go to the bus stop.

(2) My class reads a new book each week.

_____

(3) The police officer receives a medal.

_____

(4) We traveled to Mexico.

_____

(5) I cooked a delicious meal tonight.

_____

You can do it!

Verbs
Future Progressive

Date   /   /

Name

Score   /100

1 Trace the helping verb *will be*. Then complete each sentence with the present participle (*-ing* form) of the verb in the brackets.

5 points each

(1) In April, the scientists _will be studying_ fossils. [study]

(2) Mom _will be_____ during the whole vacation. [work]

(3) The talented singer _will be_____ autographs. [sign]

(4) My aunt and uncle _will be_____ us this summer. [visit]

Don't forget!

Verbs in the **future progressive tense** describe an action that will be happening over a period of time in the future. To write in the future progressive tense, use the helping verbs *will be* and the *-ing* form of the main verb.

For example: Next week we ⟨will be⟩ |studying| biology in class.

helping verbs   present participle

---

2 Complete each sentence with the helping verb *will be* and a verb from the box.

5 points each

| helping | voting | swimming | performing |

(1) She _will be voting_ in the elections in November.

(2) I _____ in the meets this fall.

(3) The juggler _____ at the fair this month.

(4) The veterinarian _____ the homeless kitten find a home.

3 Complete each question with a verb from the brackets.

4 points each

(1) Will Lana be _____ the swim team?   [joined / joining]

(2) Will they be _____ for their vacation today?   [pack / packing]

(3) Will Dad be _____ for us over the weekend?   [cooking / cooks]

(4) Will Caleb be _____ to camp with us?   [going / go]

(5) Will she be _____ her exams this year?   [take / taking]

4 Rewrite each sentence in the negative future progressive tense.

8 points each

(1) We will be going to the amusement park for vacation.

We will not be going to the
amusement park for vacation.

(2) Zola and Riku will be coming to school early.

_____

(3) The artist will be painting in his studio then.

_____

(4) You will be attending a new school this fall.

_____

(5) Our dogs will be staying in a kennel while we are gone.

_____

_____

Great effort.

Verbs
Past Progressive

23

Level
★★★

Score

/100

Date   /   /

Name

1 Trace the helping verb. Then complete each sentence with the present participle (-*ing* form) of the verb in the brackets.

5 points each

(1) The family _was_____ volleyball all afternoon.   [play]

(2) The chicks _were_____ in their nest all day.   [chirp]

(3) My uncle _was_____ when a storm blew in.   [sail]

(4) The old toys _were_____ dust in the attic.   [collect]

┌─ **Don't forget!** ───┐

Verbs in the **past progressive tense** describe an action that was continuing in the past. To write in the past progressive tense, use the helping verb *was* and the -*ing* form of the main verb.

For example: Last week, I (was) [working] on my science project.

helping verb   present participle

└──┘

2 Complete each sentence with the helping verb *was* and a verb from the box.

5 points each

listening	wearing	following	riding

(1) The dog _____ the little girl everywhere she went.

(2) I _____ to the ghost story when I started to get scared!

(3) A cowboy _____ his horse when he saw a twister coming.

(4) Madison _____ a bright yellow dress on her birthday.

3 Complete each question with a verb from the brackets.

4 points each

(1) Was Dave _____ to Toronto?

[travel / traveled / traveling]

(2) Were the boys _____ OK after the roller coaster ride?

[feel / feeling / felt]

(3) Were the electricians _____ the lights all day?

[fix / fixed / fixing]

(4) Was the toy _____ when you bought it?

[work / working / worked]

(5) Were the onions _____ in the spring?

[sprout / sprouting / sprouted]

4 Rewrite each sentence in the negative past progressive tense.

8 points each

(1) Samuel was teasing his brother during recess.

Samuel was not teasing his brother during recess.

(2) The sisters were raking leaves last weekend.

_____

(3) My favorite team was doing well last season.

_____

(4) The family was picnicking when it began to rain.

_____

(5) Her dog was pulling the leash during the walk.

_____

You've got it!

Review
Verbs

24

Level ★★★

Score

/100

Date / /

Name

1 Complete each sentence with a helping verb and main verb from the box.

5 points each

| am waiting | are exercising | are swinging | is sewing | are coloring |

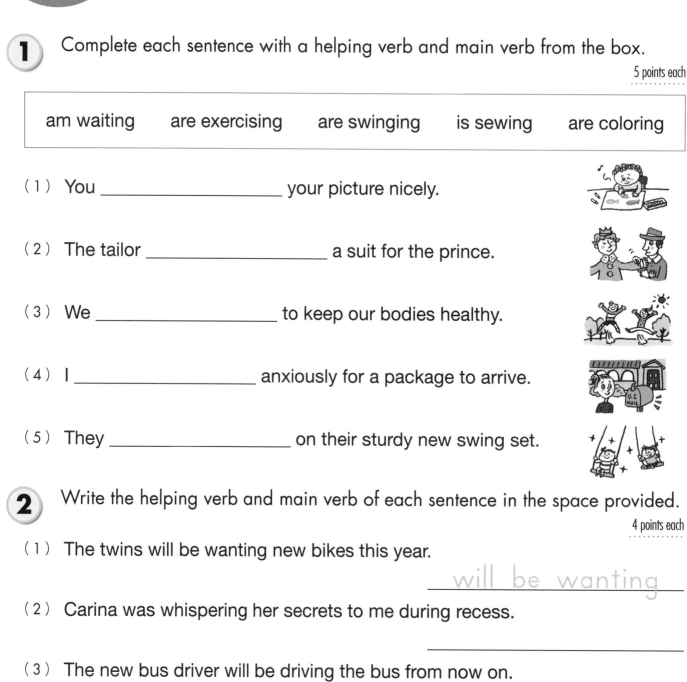

(1) You _____ your picture nicely.

(2) The tailor _____ a suit for the prince.

(3) We _____ to keep our bodies healthy.

(4) I _____ anxiously for a package to arrive.

(5) They _____ on their sturdy new swing set.

2 Write the helping verb and main verb of each sentence in the space provided.

4 points each

(1) The twins will be wanting new bikes this year.

_____will be wanting_____

(2) Carina was whispering her secrets to me during recess.

_____

(3) The new bus driver will be driving the bus from now on.

_____

(4) The architects were designing the office building for two years.

_____

(5) Monte will participate in the dance competition.

_____

3 Complete the question based on each answer.

5 points each

(1) <u>Was</u> I <u>laughing</u> too loudly?

Yes, you were laughing too loudly.

(2) _____ Uncle Huan _____ us a gift?

Yes, Uncle Huan will bring us a gift.

(3) _____ you _____ on our trip?

No, I will not be skiing on our trip.

(4) _____ I _____ with you?

Yes, you are coming with me.

4 Rewrite each sentence in the negative form.

7 points each

(1) I am going to the basketball game.

_____

(2) Darius was brushing the dog's curly hair.

_____

(3) Our pet cat will sit happily in his carrier.

_____

(4) You are decorating for the party.

_____

(5) The meteorologist was predicting rain.

_____

You went the extra mile!

Writing a Sentence
Declarative

Level ★★★

Date / /

Name

Score /100

25

1 Write a sentence with the words in brackets. Begin each sentence with a capital letter and end it with a period.

5 points each

(1) <u>Our dad is home from work.</u>

[dad / our / work / is / home / from]

(2) _____

[puppy / holds / Carson / a]

(3) _____

[stage / on / cousin / my / sings]

(4) _____

[the / plays / the / trumpet / girl]

Don't forget!

A **declarative sentence** states a fact or an idea. A declarative sentence begins with a capital letter and ends with a period.

For example: Mom made oatmeal cookies.

---

2 Write a declarative sentence with a subject and predicate from the boxes.

5 points each

Subjects	Predicates
My homemade cupcake	looks at the seashell fell on the floor
The teacher Dorothy	pointed to the incorrect answer
The worker	mines for gold

(1) _____

(2) _____

(3) _____

(4) _____

3 Write a declarative sentence with the sentence parts in the box.

5 points each

We	pushes	to the playground.
My dad	are going	me on the swing.
Basketball	watches	the clock as time runs out.
Everyone	is	an exciting sport.

(1) <u>We are going to the playground.</u>

(2) _____

(3) _____

(4) _____

4 Write a declarative sentence to match each picture. (Answers may vary.)

10 points each

(1) _____

(2) _____

(3) _____

(4) _____

Good for you!

Writing a Sentence
Interrogative

26

Level

Score

/100

Date　　/　　/

Name

1 Complete each sentence with the words in the brackets. Begin each sentence with a capital letter and end it with a question mark.

4 points each

(1) ___Is___ Mikali _ready to study?_　　[is / ready to study]

(2) _____ they _____

[are / thankful for the gift]

(3) _____ Mr. Ruiz _____

[is / feeling well]

(4) _____ we _____

[do / have time to play]

(5) _____ I _____

[may / have more berries]

> **Don't forget!**
>
> An **interrogative sentence** asks a question. An interrogative sentence begins with a capital letter and ends with a question mark.
>
> For example: Would you like some milk?

2 Rewrite each declarative sentence as a interrogative sentence. End each sentence with a question mark.

5 points each

(1) My book is here.

Is my book here?

(2) The group is crossing the street cautiously.

_____

(3) The banker is counting our money.

_____

(4) She did plant the tulip in the soil.

_____

3 Complete each interrogative sentence. End each sentence with a question mark.

6 points each

(1) __Is__ Sean _drinking a vanilla shake?_

Yes, Sean is drinking a vanilla shake.

(2) _____ the girls _____

Yes, the girls are eating ice cream.

(3) _____ Tianna _____

Yes, Tianna is taller than Dana.

(4) _____ Tianna and Dana _____

Yes, Tianna and Dana are taller than Sean.

(5) _____ Tianna _____

Yes, Tianna is taller than Dana and Sean.

4 Rewrite each declarative sentence as an interrogative sentence.

6 points each

(1) Bill does wear glasses.

Does Bill wear glasses? _____

(2) The cheetah is the fastest animal.

_____

(3) The zookeeper is taking care of the animals.

_____

(4) Turtles do spend most of their time in the water.

_____

(5) Dinosaurs did live millions of years ago.

_____

Keep it up!

Writing a Sentence
Imperative

Level ★★★

Date / /

Name

Score /100

1 Complete each sentence with words or phrases from the box. Begin each sentence with a capital letter.

5 points each

don't forget	give your	walk	get	do your

(1) _____ homework neatly.

(2) _____ parents the permission slip.

(3) _____ your backpack!

(4) _____ slowly down the hall!

(5) _____ some exercise.

Don't forget!

An **imperative sentence** makes a request or command. An imperative sentence ends with a period or an exclamation point.

For example: Please be careful crossing the street.
Watch out!

---

2 Write the imperative sentence in the space on the right.

5 points each

(1) Help me dig in the garden.
Did you dig in the garden?

Help me dig in the garden.

(2) The days are getting shorter.
Change the time on the clocks.

_____

(3) Watch out!
That bicyclist goes fast.

_____

(4) Please rake the leaves today.
The rake is in the garage.

_____

(5) We're going to the beach.
Don't forget to wear sunscreen.

_____

3 Complete each answer with a word from the box. Begin each sentence with a capital letter.

5 points each

hit	cut	put	thank	give

(1) Where can I put Jordan's birthday present?

_____ it on the table.

(2) How many slices of cake should I cut?

_____ two more slices.

(3) How do we break the colorful piñata?

_____ the piñata with the stick.

(4) What should I do with the goody bags?

_____ them to your guests.

(5) What should we do at the end?

_____ all your friends for coming.

4 Write an imperative sentence with the words in the brackets.

5 points each

(1) [get / please / me / a / pizza / slice / of]

Please get me a slice of pizza.

(2) [dishes / stack / the]

_____

(3) [complete / homework / your]

_____

(4) [this / present / give / Mrs. / Song / to]

_____

(5) [cake / the / eat / batter / don't]

_____

_____

Two thumbs up!

55

Writing a Sentence
Exclamatory

28

Level ★★★

Date / /

Name

Score /100

1 Rewrite each sentence with an exclamation point at the end.

5 points each

(1) I am very forgetful.

I am very forgetful!

(2) We are going to the beach.

_____

(3) I knocked over Aunt Cicely's vase.

_____

(4) That movie was amazing.

_____

> **Don't forget!**
>
> An **exclamatory sentence** shows strong feeling. An exclamatory sentence ends with an exclamation point.
>   For example: Snow is falling*!*

2 Complete each exclamatory sentence with a word from the box. End each sentence with an exclamation point.

6 points each

| hurts | riding | fell | fantastic | spotted |

(1) I love _____ my bike __

(2) My eye _____ __

(3) Doug _____ an eagle __

(4) You did a _____ job __

(5) I almost _____ into the water __

3 Rewrite each exclamatory sentence with capitalization, spacing, and punctuation.

6 points each

(1) theyaretalkingtooloudly

They are talking too loudly!

(2) weareinvitedtoacelebration

_____

(3) thatpaintingisstunning

_____

(4) thesechildrenareveryrespectful

_____

(5) myskatesareskidding

_____

4 Write an exclamatory sentence based on each illustration. (Answers may vary.)

5 points each

(1) _____

(2) _____

(3) _____

(4) _____

You're sharp!

Describing an Object

Date   /   /

Name

Score
/100

1 Read each description. Match each description with the name of an object from the box.

3 points each

| elephant | puppy | parachute | basketball | pizza |

(1) It is round. You throw it into a hoop. _____

(2) It has floppy ears, a tail, and soft fur. _____

(3) It is round. It can have different toppings. _____

(4) It is enormous. It has gray, wrinkly skin. _____

(5) It is large and made of cloth. A skydiver uses it. _____

Hint: Adjectives describe color, size, shape, texture, smell, and taste.
For example: My big birthday cake was pink and round with sweet icing.

2 Complete the passage with adjectives from the box.

7 points each

| green | round | fragrant | tall | back |

The Kim family's home has a (1) _____ roof,

a (2) _____ pool in the backyard, and a large

(3) _____ porch. Mr. and Mrs. Kim plant

(4) _____ trees and (5) _____ flowers

in the yard.

3

Complete the passage with adjectives to match the picture. (Answers may vary.)

5 points each

I love my local park. I go there every weekend, even if it rains. It has a swing

set with a (1) _____ slide and a (2) _____ tree house. There

are (3) _____ -smelling flowers on top of a (4) _____ hill.

I play basketball in the (5) _____ sport court. We bring our

(6) _____ jump ropes and (7) _____ soccer balls. The

(8) _____ grass tickles our feet as we play. All the neighborhood kids

come to play together.

4

Describe the object in three sentences. (Answers may vary.)

10 points for completion

This guitar is _____

_____

_____

_____

_____

Very creative!

Describing an Event

Date   /   /

Name

Score
/ 100

1 Trace each word to complete the paragraph.

5 points each

I am helping Mom do the dishes.

(1) _First,_ I put the dishes into the soapy water.

(2) _Next,_ Mom wipes them with her sponge.

(3) _Then,_ I rinse them in hot, steamy water.

(4) _Finally,_ we place them carefully in the dish rack.

Mom says that I am an excellent helper!

┌─ **Don't forget!** ─────────────────────────────────────┐

The **sequence** is the order in which things happen. Use signal words like *first, next, then, after,* and *finally* to describe the sequence of events.

└───┘

2 Complete each sentence with a signal word from the box.

5 points each

next	first	after	finally	before

Leah gets ready for school each weekday morning. (1) _____, she

chooses her outfit, gets dressed, and brushes her teeth. (2) _____, she

walks downstairs and eats a healthy breakfast. (3) _____ breakfast, she

collects her lunch box, backpack, and jacket. (4) _____ she leaves, she

says good-bye to her pet snake. (5) _____, she goes outside to wait at

the bus stop.

3 Describe the event by putting the sentences from the box in order.

5 points each

> First, they put the ingredients on the counter.
> Finally, they put the two sides together.
> Then, they added lettuce and onion.　At last, they sat down to eat.
> Second, they put mustard on the bread.
> After the vegetables, they added meat.

Eddy and Mino made lunch.

(1) First, they put the ingredients on the counter.

(2) _____

(3) _____

(4) _____

(5) _____

(6) _____

4 Describe the event by putting the sentences from the box in order.

5 points each

> Next, we lifted Beamer into the bath.
> Then, Dad scrubbed him with shampoo.
> Finally, we dried and brushed him.
> After the shampoo, we rinsed him.
> First, we filled the tub with water.

Yesterday, we gave our dog Beamer a bath.

(1) _____

(2) _____

(3) _____

(4) _____

(5) _____

Way to go!

Writing a Paragraph
Objects

31

Level ★★★

Date / /

Name

Score /100

1 Complete each sentence with an adjective from the box.

5 points each

| green | tasty | hot | thick | gooey | large |

My grandmother made my favorite dish—lasagna!

(1) A _____ piece sat on my plate.

(2) It had a _____ red sauce.

(3) She put garlic, mushrooms, and _____ peppers inside.

(4) The _____ cheese stretched out when I took a forkful.

(5) Steam rose from it, so it was too _____ to eat right away.

(6) When it finally cooled, I took a nibble, and it was _____!

Don't forget!

A **paragraph** is an organized piece of writing that discusses a topic or event. The first sentence of a paragraph is **indented**, or set away from the margin.

2 Rewrite the sentences from the exercise above in paragraph form. Indent the first sentence.

20 points for completion

_____My grandmother made my favorite dish— lasagna!_____

_____

_____

_____

_____

3 Complete each sentence with a word from the box.

5 points each

| green | birthday | top | vanilla | sixth |

Happy Birthday

(1) Today is my sister's _____ birthday.

(2) Dad and I decided to bake her a _____ cake.

(3) Her favorite flavors are chocolate cake with _____ icing.

(4) We made it in a round pan, and when it was done, we scattered _____ sprinkles over it.

(5) Dad added six candles on _____, and then he lit them.

My sister was excited when she saw how beautiful it looked!

4 Rewrite the sentences from the exercise above in paragraph form. Indent the first sentence.

25 points for completion

_____

_____

_____

_____

_____

_____

_____

Wonderful work!

Writing a Paragraph
Event

32

Level ★★★

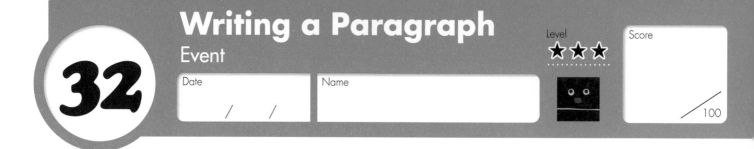

Date / /

Name

Score /100

1 Complete the paragraph with words from the box.

5 points each

home	bag	crying	the beach	sparkly	happy
	last year	gold necklace	charm	owner	

(1) _____, while on vacation at (2) _____ with my grandparents, I found treasure. I was digging in the gritty sand when I noticed something (3) _____. It was a (4) _____ with a star-shaped (5) _____. I walked up and down the beach to ask if anyone was the (6) _____, but no one was. My grandfather said it was time to go home, so I put the necklace safely in my (7) _____. On the way (8) _____, I saw a girl (9) _____ to her mother. I ran up to the girl and asked if she had lost a necklace. She had! When I pulled it out of my bag, she was so (10) _____ that she jumped up and down for joy.

Don't forget!

Narrative writing is writing about an event. A **narrative** tells a story about a real or imaginary event. A narrative should include a beginning, a middle, and an end.

┌─ Beginning   ┌─ Middle

For example: Yesterday, my friend Elton and I were at the park. Elton said that he was the king of the playground, and we pretended that I was the knight guarding his castle. We had a lot of fun and went home when it got dark.
      └─ End

2 Complete each part of the narrative with words from the box.

5 points each

played	clapped	backstage	sat	breath

Beginning

Who: Ana

What: her piano recital

Where: (1) _____

Middle

She took a deep (2) _____ and looked for her parents in the audience.

Ana stepped on stage and (3) _____ on the piano bench.

She opened her music and (4) _____ her piece perfectly!

End

Everyone (5) _____ and cheered as Ana took a bow.

3 Use the chart above to write a paragraph. Indent the first sentence.

25 points for completion

_____ Ana was backstage for her piano recital. _____

_____

_____

_____

_____

Remarkable!

33

1 Complete the paragraph with words from the box.

4 points each

| green and white   friendly   excellent   swiftly   middle school |

Gabriella is my favorite cousin. She is a star on her (1) _____

soccer team. She runs down the field (2) _____ in her (3) _____

uniform. Gabriella is an (4) _____ student too. She studies very hard,

and she loves to read. Gabriella is also a lot of fun. She is (5) _____ to

everyone and has many friends. I want to be just like Gabriella when I am older.

Don't forget!
When writing a paragraph about a person,
describe how that person looks and behaves.

2 Answer each question based on the passage above.

5 points each

(1) How does Gabriella run?

_____

(2) Is Gabriella an excellent or a bad student?

_____

(3) Is Gabriella friendly or unfriendly?

_____

(4) What color is Gabriella's soccer uniform?

_____

3 Answer each question according to the picture. (Answers may vary.) 5 points each

(1) Who is this person?

This person is a magician.

(2) What color is his cape?

_____

(3) What is on his hat?

_____

(4) Is his hair curly or straight?

_____

(5) Where is this person?

_____

(6) What is this person holding?

_____

4 Complete the paragraph with details from the questions and picture above.

5 points each

An old (1) _____ came to my house for my (2) _____.

He had (3) _____ hair and a beard that was tied in a knot. He wore a

flowing (4) _____ cape and a top hat with a (5) _____ star on it.

The magician was serious at first. He did not say anything—not even "Happy

birthday." Instead, he walked in and waved his magic (6) _____. Music

started playing, and then the magician made my birthday cake float through

the air!

Very nice!

Writing Two Paragraphs
Place

34

Level ★★★

Score

Date / /

Name

/100

1 Complete the paragraphs with words from the box.

5 points each

middle	creamy	look	warm	happy	shaped

At the bakery, the heat of the oven and smell of the (1) _____ bread fill

the air. A cake stand is in the (2) _____ of the room. The bakers display

cookies that are (3) _____ like animals and birds. You can hear the excited

voices of (4) _____ customers.

We (5) _____ at all the choices and choose our favorite. I pick a fluffy

doughnut with (6) _____ chocolate icing. It is a treat to visit the bakery.

Don't forget!

When describing a place, use details that are detected by the five senses (sight, smell, hearing, taste, and touch) to paint a picture in the reader's mind.

                        touch   sight   smell

For example: The soccer field has **thick green** grass. The air smells **fresh**. When we play, people cheer **loudly**. Afterward, we drink **sweet** lemonade. Yum!

                      hearing   taste

---

2 Answer each question based on the passage above.

5 points each

(1) What does the bakery smell like?

_____

(2) How are the cookies shaped?

_____

(3) What can you hear inside the bakery?

_____

(4) What does the writer's favorite doughnut feel like?

_____

3 Complete the paragraphs with the information in the chart.

5 points each

Sight	brightly colored flowers
Hearing	birds singing
Smell	freshly cut grass
Touch	warm sunshine
Taste	crisp apples

Our family works very hard on the garden in our backyard. We plant

(1) _____ so that butterflies will come. My father

likes to cut the dark, cool green grass short so we can play soccer.

After we are finished working, we like to sit and listen to the (2) _____

_____. The (3) _____ smells clean and sweet.

We play soccer in the (4) _____ and then snack on

(5) _____ from our apple tree. We love our garden.

4 Write two paragraphs describing the lunchroom. Include details detected by each of the five senses. (Answers may vary.)

25 points for completion

_____

_____

_____

_____

_____

_____

_____

— Don't forget!

When you write two paragraphs, each should have a new idea about the same topic. Also, the first line of each paragraph must be indented.

If you would like to write more, you can continue on lined paper.

35 **Review**

Level
★ ★

Score

/100

Date / /

Name

1 Rewrite each sentence with capitalization and punctuation.

5 points each

(1) the girls lucky bracelet was on her arm

_____

(2) a kangaroo was close so we stood very still

_____

(3) my mom cooked and we set the table

_____

(4) the reporter asked what did you see

_____

(5) please dont disturb others the librarian whispered

_____

2 Complete each sentence with a verb from the brackets.

5 points each

(1) The kayakers _____ wearing life jackets.   [are / is]

(2) Some people _____ afraid of spiders.   [are / is]

(3) Somebody _____ playing the trumpet nearby.   [are / is]

(4) Everyone _____ attending the assembly.   [are / is]

(5) No one _____ winning. The score is zero to zero.   [are / is]

3 Complete each sentence with the past tense of the verb in the brackets.

5 points each

(1) The spider _____ a web.

[spins]

(2) We _____ the recipe by two and baked two batches.

[multiply]

(3) They _____ at summer camp and became friends.

[meet]

(4) I _____ happy and proud at my graduation.

[feel]

(5) Her arm _____, so she wore a sling.

[hurts]

4 Complete each question.

5 points each

(1) _____ they _____ the car together?

Yes, they are repairing the car together.

(2) _____ the ballerina _____ on pointe shoes?

No, the ballerina will not twirl on pointe shoes.

(3) _____ you _____ your famous casserole tonight?

Yes, I will be baking my famous casserole tonight.

(4) _____ she _____ down her thoughts in her journal?

Yes, she has been jotting down her thoughts in her journal.

(5) _____ Rachel _____ with us on the field trip?

No, Rachel will not be riding with us on the field trip.

You're almost
at the finish line!

36 Review

Level ★★

Score

/100

Date / /

Name

1 Complete each sentence with words from the brackets.

4 points each

(1) The kittens _____ in their new basket.

[is sleeping / are sleeping]

(2) I _____ some healthy snacks.

[am making / are making]

(3) It _____ outside right now!

[are snowing / is snowing]

(4) We _____ our hiding places.

[are finding / am finding]

(5) Your friends _____ down the slide.

[is sliding / are sliding]

2 Complete each answer with the verb in the future tense.

4 points each

(1) Will your new puppy like his new toy?
Yes, he _____ his new toy.

(2) Will the scientist study the dinosaur fossils?
Yes, the scientist _____ the dinosaur fossils.

(3) Will we eat cookies after lunch?
No, we _____ not _____ cookies after lunch.

(4) Will Meier come with us to the zoo?
No, Meier _____ not _____ with us to the zoo.

(5) Will the tadpole become a frog?
Yes, the tadpole _____ a frog.

3 Rewrite each sentence in the future progressive tense.

4 points each

(1) Zoe swims while on vacation.

_____

(2) I play with my cousins at the reunion.

_____

(3) They cook dinner for everyone.

_____

(4) Dennis writes two paragraphs about his mother.

_____

(5) The men hike up the steep trail.

_____

4 Write whether each sentence is declarative, interrogative, imperative, or exclamatory.

5 points each

(1) Are you ready to go to school? _____

(2) I see a beautiful rainbow! _____

(3) Give this to Grandma, please. _____

(4) This is my best friend, Jamal. _____

(5) Be careful when you cross the street. _____

(6) Is this your essay? _____

(7) The band members write their own songs. _____

(8) Put the cupcakes on the dessert table. _____

Congratulations!
You finished!

1 Prefixes
pp 2,3

1. (1) re / redo (2) un / untie
(3) sub / subzero (4) mis / mismatch
(5) pre / preview (6) dis / dislike

2. (1) mis (2) sub (3) dis (4) pre

3. (1) unload (2) reload (3) unwrap (4) rewrap

4. (1) untie (2) dislikes (3) unload
(4) misspell (5) subzero (6) preheat

2 Suffixes
pp 4,5

1. (1) correctly (2) loud (3) quietly
(4) slowly (5) swift

2. (1) kind / kindly (2) cautious / cautiously
(3) wild / wildly (4) bright / brightly
(5) anxious / anxiously

3. (1) builds skillfully (2) colors messily
(3) steals greedily (4) work busily
(5) decorates carefully

4. (1) carefully (2) skillfully (3) messily
(4) greedily

3 Suffixes
pp 6,7

1. (1) colors / colorful / colorless
(2) care / careful / careless
(3) grace / graceful / graceless
(4) thank / thankful / thankless

2. (1) graceful (2) fearless (3) thankful (4) care

3. (1) strong / stronger / strongest
(2) young / younger / youngest
(3) easy / easier / easiest
(4) high / higher / highest (5) light / lighter / lightest

4. (1) higher / highest (2) light / lighter
(3) easy / easiest (4) strong / strongest
(5) younger / youngest

4 Indefinite Pronouns
pp 8,9

1. (1) either (2) another (3) anyone
(4) some (5) Everyone

2. (1) anyone (2) everyone (3) Either
(4) another (5) some

3. (1) another (2) everyone (3) anyone
(4) some (5) either

4. (1) everyone (2) another (3) some
(4) either (5) anyone

5 Punctuation: Speech
pp 10,11

1. (1) ," / ." (2) " / ," (3) " / ?" (4) " / ," (5) ," / ?"

2. (1) ," / ." (2) ," / ?" (3) " / ?" (4) " / ," (5) " / ,"

3. (1) Jonah said, "I will miss practice."
(2) The announcer said, "There are only five tickets."
(3) Leslie asked, "Who is the new principal?"
(4) Pete said, "These are my pet hamsters."

4. (1) "May I buy some tulips?" the man asked.
(2) Rachel told me, "I sold muffins at the bake sale."
(3) Mr. Nielsen said, "The picnic starts at eleven o'clock."
(4) Karen asked the coach, "Can we practice slap shots?"
(5) "The club meets here," she said.

6 Punctuation: Commas
pp 12,13

1. (1) The musician could play guitar, piano, and bass.
(2) Colleen likes to read novels, short stories, and news articles.
(3) My favorite foods are watermelon, corn, and ice cream.
(4) My dad packed his suit, tie, shoes, and laptop for his business trip.
(5) Humans, mice, dolphins, and chimpanzees are all mammals.

2. (1) She is not short, strong, or fast.
(2) Rita bought bread, cheese, and tomatoes.
(3) I visited Santa Fe, Madison, and Little Rock.
(4) Geckos, snakes, and sea turtles are reptiles.
(5) Daniel doesn't eat chips, soda, or chocolate.

3 (1) , and he bought a scooter
(2) , but the flies were already inside
(3) , so she joined a team
(4) , but the clay was not dry
(5) , yet the man didn't get on it

4 (1) I will win, or it will be a tie.
(2) Birds must protect their chicks, so they stay near their nests.
(3) The man walked the dog, and the woman trained it.
(4) The store had books to sell, but there were no customers.
(5) He told me to wait, yet I left anyway.

7 Punctuation: Possessives   pp 14, 15

1 (1) 's   (2) 's   (3) 's   (4) 's   (5) 's

2 (1) 's   (2) 's   (3) 's   (4) 's   (5) 's

3 (1) The mailman's glasses are thick.
(2) The tourist's sneakers are comfortable.
(3) The captain's ferry is blue.
(4) Allan's birdhouse is outside.
(5) Ellen's job is at a camp.

4 (1) That is Prateek's lunch bag.
(2) Those are Raymond's books.
(3) That is Ellen's volleyball.
(4) That is Megan's backpack.
(5) Those are Ryan's rain boots.

8 Review: Punctuation   pp 16, 17

1 (1) Georgia said, "I like your comic."
(2) My teacher said, "Please be on time."
(3) "Will you call the king?" the queen asked.
(4) "A hurricane is on the way," the news anchor reported.
(5) Grandma asked, "Did you like this book?"

2 (1) , or Dad will order pizza
(2) , yet I was still nervous
(3) , but he is tired now
(4) , so we will need supplies
(5) , and Micah unpacked them

3 (1) The janitor's mop is wet.
(2) The figure skater's costume is beautiful.
(3) My cousin's rosebush is red.
(4) Amy's apron is large.
(5) The basketball player's game is important.

4 (1) The farmer sold berries, and his son sold lemons.
(2) "Did you hear the news?" Karen asked.
(3) A ballerina's pointe shoes help her stand on her toes.
(4) "The science club's projects are on display," the principal said.

9 Subject / Predicate: Review   pp 18, 19

1 (1) The birds / escape from the cage
(2) My brother / taught me fractions
(3) A bandit / stole the horse
(4) Ms. Alvarez / baked ten cookies
(5) Jess and Ed / tossed a ball

2 (1) The powerful gardener lifted the branches.
(2) The clever scientist showed his invention.
(3) Alice's colorful kite is tangled in the tree.
(4) The blaring alarm hurts my ears.

3 (1) The trick-or-treaters
(2) My pink gloves
(3) A graceful giraffe
(4) The jubilant team
(5) Our cautious bus driver

4 (1) passed me the vegetables
(2) shopped at the market
(3) lit a candle and led the guests
(4) wandered on the hill
(5) littered the beach

10 Subject / Predicate: Review   pp 20, 21

1 (1) gleefully   (2) everywhere   (3) easily
(4) far   (5) today

2 (1) went to the bathroom to carefully wash my hands
(2) briskly walked to his golf ball
(3) kindheartedly made me soup when I was sick
(4) nervously walked to the piano to perform at the recital
(5) silently put the books on the shelf

3 (1) rapidly ran after the elephant
(2) knew every answer on the science test
(3) is turning nine years old soon
(4) accidentally spilled his drink
(5) stayed up late to watch the stars

4 (1) (An adventurous fish) / swam through the ocean

(2) (The bland potatoes) / stuck to the top of his mouth

(3) (Jed) / energetically ran to catch the ice-cream truck

(4) (The eager dog) / impatiently waited for some scraps

11 Subject / Verb / Object
pp 22, 23

1 (1) (Stacey) / plays / the accordion

(2) (The worker) / constructs / a home

(3) (My mom) / made / a pie

(4) (We) / watch / the acrobats

(5) (The bear) / caught / a fish

2 (1) The ball / shattered / the window

(2) I / ignored / the bully

(3) Matt / trained / his dog

(4) The president / wrote / a letter

3 (1) The teacher / borrowed / a pencil

(2) We / ride / the carousel

(3) The car / hit / the curb

(4) My doctor / treated / my wound

(5) The friends / collected / seashells

4 (1) is carrying / an umbrella

(2) The man / a horse

(3) is writing

(4) The girl / a helmet

(5) The boys / are trading / baseball cards

12 Subject / Verb / Object
pp 24, 25

1 (1) Doug and the coach / brought / the bats

(2) The tall woman / rode / a motorcycle

(3) The famous athlete / fractured / her arm

(4) Her husband / cooked / her dinner

(5) Marie and her friend / moved / the wardrobe

2 (1) the forest   (2) the carrots   (3) a camera

(4) the eggplant   (5) the paper

3 (1) sunblock and hats

(2) The enormous octopus

(3) a woman and two bags

(4) Carrie and Ryan

4 (1) Tammy / cut / tomatoes

(2) The firefighter / carried / a hose

(3) Ava / took / her lunch

(4) The detective / found / a clue

13 Subject and Verb Agreement
pp 26, 27

1 (1) practice   (2) pulls   (3) are

(4) spend   (5) costs

2 (1) alien   (2) actor   (3) horses

(4) feather

3 (1) am / are   (2) are / is   (3) is / are

(4) Are / is

4 (1) wash   (2) use   (3) drops

(4) signs   (5) overflow   (6) become

(7) Is

14 Subject and Verb Agreement
pp 28, 29

1 [Singular subjects]

Each / Everyone / Somebody / No one / Anybody

[Plural subjects]

Both / Several / Few / Many

2 (1) know   (2) rots   (3) sketches

(4) perform   (5) want   (6) were

(7) realizes   (8) compete

3 (1) are   (2) are   (3) is

(4) is   (5) are   (6) is

(7) is   (8) is   (9) is

15 Verbs: Past Tense
pp 30, 31

1 (1) showed   (2) whispered   (3) wrapped

(4) sewed   (5) switched

2 (1) counted   (2) traveled   (3) ended

(4) hovered   (5) glowed

3 [Present]

shave

[Past]

tickled / measured / competed

4 (1) a) wiped   b) wipe

(2) a) shaved   b) shaves

(3) a) tickled   b) tickles

(4) a) measured   b) measure

(5) a) competed   b) competes

16 Irregular Verbs: Past Tense pp 32,33

1 (1) multiplied (2) cried (3) carried
(4) tidied (5) studied

2 (1) carried (2) multiply (3) cry
(4) studied (5) tidy

3 swept / slept / met / felt / crept

4 (1) a) met   b) meet   (2) a) slept   b) sleep
(3) a) felt   b) feel   (4) a) swept   b) sweep
(5) a) crept   b) creep

17 Irregular Verbs: Past Tense pp 34,35

1 (1) dug (2) spun (3) swung
(4) stuck (5) hung

2 (1) stick (2) dig (3) hung
(4) swung (5) spin

3 hurt / put / spread / cost / burst

4 (1) a) spread   b) spread   (2) a) cost   b) cost
(3) a) put   b) put   (4) a) hurt   b) hurt
(5) a) burst   b) burst

18 Irregular Verbs: Past Tense pp 36,37

1 (1) was (2) were (3) was (4) did (5) had

2 (1) was (2) are (3) were (4) did (5) has

3 was / was / did / had / were

4 (1) a) had   b) have   (2) a) was   b) is
(3) a) were   b) are   (4) a) did   b) do
(5) a) was   b) am

19 Verbs: Present Progressive pp 38,39

1 (1) is sleeping (2) am licking
(3) are riding (4) are watching

2 (1) going (2) reading (3) planting
(4) playing

3 (1) is reading (2) are going (3) am talking
(4) is singing (5) are writing

4 (1) is checking our book reports
(2) are riding our bicycles home
(3) am redoing my messy homework
(4) are having a barbecue
(5) is running a marathon

20 Verbs: Present Progressive pp 40,41

1 (1) am walking (2) is working
(3) are cheering (4) is crying

2 (1) I am not singing with the choir tonight.
(2) Annika is not playing in the championship.
(3) They are not sitting in the theater.
(4) The baker is not baking cupcakes.

3 (1) Are / listening (2) Are / working
(3) Is / speaking (4) Am / doing

4 (1) Are (2) is (3) are (4) Am (5) is (6) am

21 Verbs: Future Tense pp 42,43

1 (1) will send (2) will think (3) will lay
(4) will work

2 (1) will / practice (2) will / build (3) will / arrive
(4) will / drive (5) will / bake

3 (1) will play (2) will / eat (3) will sing
(4) will / take

4 (1) Raj will go to the bus stop.
(2) My class will read a new book each week.
(3) The police officer will receive a medal.
(4) We will travel to Mexico.
(5) I will cook a delicious meal tonight.

22 Verbs: Future Progressive pp 44,45

1 (1) will be studying (2) will be working
(3) will be signing (4) will be visiting

2 (1) will be voting (2) will be swimming
(3) will be performing (4) will be helping

3 (1) joining (2) packing (3) cooking
(4) going (5) taking

4 (1) We will not be going to the amusement park for
vacation.
(2) Zola and Riku will not be coming to school early.
(3) The artist will not be painting in his studio then.
(4) You will not be attending a new school this fall.
(5) Our dogs will not be staying in a kennel while we
are gone.

23 Verbs: Past Progressive
pp 46,47

1 (1) was playing   (2) were chirping
(3) was sailing   (4) were collecting

2 (1) was following   (2) was listening
(3) was riding   (4) was wearing

3 (1) traveling   (2) feeling   (3) fixing
(4) working   (5) sprouting

4 (1) Samuel was not teasing his brother during recess.
(2) The sisters were not raking leaves last weekend.
(3) My favorite team was not doing well last season.
(4) The family was not picnicking when it began to rain.
(5) Her dog was not pulling the leash during the walk.

24 Review: Verbs
pp 48,49

1 (1) are coloring   (2) is sewing
(3) are exercising   (4) am waiting
(5) are swinging

2 (1) will be wanting   (2) was whispering
(3) will be driving   (4) were designing
(5) will participate

3 (1) Was / laughing   (2) Will / bring
(3) Will / be skiing   (4) Am / coming

4 (1) I am not going to the basketball game.
(2) Darius was not brushing the dog's curly hair.
(3) Our pet cat will not sit happily in his carrier.
(4) You are not decorating for the party.
(5) The meteorologist was not predicting rain.

25 Writing a Sentence: Declarative
pp 50,51

1 (1) Our dad is home from work.
(2) Carson holds a puppy.
(3) My cousin sings on stage.
(4) The girl plays the trumpet.

2 (1) My homemade cupcake fell on the floor.
(2) The teacher pointed to the incorrect answer.
(3) Dorothy looks at the seashell.
(4) The worker mines for gold.

3 (1) We are going to the playground.
(2) My dad pushes me on the swing.
(3) Basketball is an exciting sport.
(4) Everyone watches the clock as time runs out.

4 [SAMPLE ANSWERS]
(1) The soccer team won the game.
(2) I go to elementary school.
(3) Pizza is my favorite food.
(4) We went to the beach for vacation.

26 Writing a Sentence: Interrogative
pp 52,53

1 (1) Is / ready to study?
(2) Are / thankful for the gift?
(3) Is / feeling well?
(4) Do / have time to play?
(5) May / have more berries?

2 (1) Is my book here?
(2) Is the group crossing the street cautiously?
(3) Is the banker counting our money?
(4) Did she plant the tulip in the soil?

3 (1) Is / drinking a vanilla shake?
(2) Are / eating ice cream?
(3) Is / taller than Dana?
(4) Are / taller than Sean?
(5) Is / taller than Dana and Sean?

4 (1) Does Bill wear glasses?
(2) Is the cheetah the fastest animal?
(3) Is the zookeeper taking care of the animals?
(4) Do turtles spend most of their time in the water?
(5) Did dinosaurs live millions of years ago?

27 Writing a Sentence: Imperative
pp 54,55

1 (1) Do your   (2) Give your   (3) Don't forget
(4) Walk   (5) Get

2 (1) Help me dig in the garden.
(2) Change the time on the clocks.
(3) Watch out!
(4) Please rake the leaves today.
(5) Don't forget to wear sunscreen.

3 (1) Put   (2) Cut   (3) Hit   (4) Give   (5) Thank

4 (1) Please get me a slice of pizza.
(2) Stack the dishes.
(3) Complete your homework.
(4) Give this present to Mrs. Song.
(5) Don't eat the cake batter.

28 Writing a Sentence: Exclamatory pp 56,57

1 (1) I am very forgetful!
(2) We are going to the beach!
(3) I knocked over Aunt Cicely's vase!
(4) That movie was amazing!

2 (1) riding / ! (2) hurts / ! (3) spotted / !
(4) fantastic / ! (5) fell / !

3 (1) They are talking too loudly!
(2) We are invited to a celebration!
(3) That painting is stunning!
(4) These children are very respectful!
(5) My skates are skidding!

4 [SAMPLE ANSWERS]
(1) I got an A on my science test!
(2) Crossing the street can be dangerous!
(3) The huge storm knocked our tree down!
(4) Our basketball team won the championship!

29 Describing an Object pp 58,59

1 (1) basketball (2) puppy (3) pizza
(4) elephant (5) parachute

2 (1) green (2) round (3) back
(4) tall (5) fragrant

3 [SAMPLE ANSWERS]
(1) curvy (2) large (3) sweet
(4) steep (5) rectangular (6) long
(7) black and white (8) short

4 [SAMPLE ANSWER]
This guitar is shiny and green. It has six strings.
The neck is black.

30 Describing an Event pp 60,61

1 (1) First, (2) Next, (3) Then, (4) Finally,

2 (1) First (2) Next (3) After (4) Before
(5) Finally

3 (1) First, they put the ingredients on the counter.
(2) Second, they put mustard on the bread.
(3) Then, they added lettuce and onion.
(4) After the vegetables, they added meat.
(5) Finally, they put the two sides together.
(6) At last, they sat down to eat.

4 (1) First, we filled the tub with water.
(2) Next, we lifted Beamer into the bath.
(3) Then, Dad scrubbed him with shampoo.
(4) After the shampoo, we rinsed him.
(5) Finally, we dried and brushed him.

31 Writing a Paragraph: Objects pp 62,63

1 (1) large (2) thick (3) green
(4) gooey (5) hot (6) tasty

2 My grandmother made my favorite dish—lasagna!
A large piece sat on my plate. It had a thick red
sauce. She put garlic, mushrooms, and green
peppers inside. The gooey cheese stretched out
when I took a fork full. Steam rose from it, so it was too
hot to eat right away. When it finally cooled, I took a
nibble, and it was tasty!

3 (1) sixth (2) birthday (3) vanilla
(4) green (5) top

4 Today is my sister's sixth birthday. Dad and I
decided to bake her a birthday cake. Her favorite
flavors are chocolate cake with vanilla icing. We made
it in a round pan, and when it was done, we scattered
green sprinkles over it. Dad added six candles on
top, and then he lit them. My sister was excited when
she saw how beautiful it looked!

32 Writing a Paragraph: Event pp 64,65

1 (1) Last year (2) the beach (3) sparkly
(4) gold necklace (5) charm (6) owner
(7) bag (8) home (9) crying
(10) happy

2 (1) backstage (2) breath (3) sat
(4) played (5) clapped

3 Ana was backstage for her piano recital. She took a
deep breath and looked for her parents in the
audience. Ana stepped on stage and sat on the piano
bench. She opened her music and played her piece
perfectly! Everyone clapped and cheered as Ana
took a bow.

33 Writing a Paragraph: Person pp 66,67

1 (1) middle school   (2) swiftly
(3) green and white   (4) excellent
(5) friendly

2 (1) Gabriella runs swiftly.
(2) Gabriella is an excellent student.
(3) Gabriella is friendly.
(4) Gabriella's soccer uniform is green and white.

3 (1) This person is a magician.
[SAMPLE ANSWERS]
(2) His cape is black.
(3) A green star is on his hat.
(4) His hair is curly.
(5) This person is at a birthday party.
(6) This person is holding a magic wand.

4 (1) magician   (2) birthday party   (3) curly
(4) black   (5) green   (6) wand

34 Writing Two Paragraphs: Place pp 68,69

1 (1) warm   (2) middle   (3) shaped
(4) happy   (5) look   (6) creamy

2 (1) The bakery smells like warm bread.
(2) The cookies are shaped like animals and birds.
(3) You can hear the excited voices of happy customers.
(4) The writer's favorite doughnut feels fluffy.

3 (1) brightly colored flowers
(2) birds singing
(3) freshly cut grass
(4) warm sunshine
(5) crisp apples

4 [SAMPLE ANSWER]
    In the cafeteria, there are many tables with gray chairs. You can hear the students talking to one another. The students are happy that it is lunchtime.
    The room smells like the tacos that are being served for lunch. The taco shells are crunchy. The milk is very cold. Lunch is delicious!

35 Review pp 70,71

1 (1) The girl's lucky bracelet was on her arm.
(2) A kangaroo was close, so we stood very still.
(3) My mom cooked, and we set the table.
(4) The reporter asked, "What did you see?"
(5) "Please don't disturb others," the librarian whispered.

2 (1) are   (2) are   (3) is   (4) is   (5) is

3 (1) spun   (2) multiplied   (3) met
(4) felt   (5) hurt

4 (1) Are / repairing   (2) Will / twirl
(3) Will / be baking   (4) Has / been jotting
(5) Will / be riding

36 Review pp 72,73

1 (1) are sleeping   (2) am making
(3) is snowing   (4) are finding
(5) are sliding

2 (1) will like   (2) will study
(3) will / eat   (4) will / come
(5) will become

3 (1) Zoe will be swimming while on vacation.
(2) I will be playing with my cousins at the reunion.
(3) They will be cooking dinner for everyone.
(4) Dennis will be writing two paragraphs about his mother.
(5) The men will be hiking up the steep trail.

4 (1) Interrogative   (2) Exclamatory
(3) Imperative   (4) Declarative
(5) Imperative   (6) Interrogative
(7) Declarative   (8) Imperative